Time

This math series is dedicated to Nick, Tony, Riley, and Hailey.

Published by The Child's World®
PO Box 326
Chanhassen, MN 55317-0326
800-599-READ
www.childsworld.com

Design and Production: The Creative Spark, San Juan Capistrano, CA
Photos: All photography © David M. Budd Photography except p. 23,
All rights reserved, Photo Archives, Denver Museum of Nature & Science.

Library of Congress Cataloging-in-Publication Data
Pistoia, Sara.
  Time / by Sara Pistoia.
       p. cm. — (Mighty math series)
Includes index.
Summary: Simple text introduces the concept of time and how time is
measured using the sun, calendars, clocks, watches, and timers.
  ISBN 1-56766-118-1 (lib. bdg. : alk. paper)
 1. Time measurements—Juvenile literature. [1. Time measurements. 2.
Time.] I. Title. II. Series.
  QB209.5 .P57 2002
  529'.7—dc21
                                        2002005347

MIGHTY MATH

Time

Sara Pistoia

The Child's World

Time is the passage of seconds, minutes, hours, days, months, and years. A year is the time it takes the earth to travel around the sun one time.

We use calendars to keep track of each year in months, weeks, and days. There are twelve months in the year: January, February, March, April, May, June, July, August, September, October, November, and December.

Hi! I'm Math Mutt! I'm here to help you learn about time.

Did you already have your birthday this year? Look on a calendar to count the months until your next one. As it gets closer, you can count the weeks and days!

I wish I could have a birthday in every month of the year!

There are four weeks in each month. There are seven days in each week.

And there are twenty-four hours in a day.

Can you name the days of the week? I can!
Sunday, Monday, Tuesday, Wednesday,
Thursday, Friday, and Saturday!

9

Your teacher can use a calendar to tell you when your next test will be. You'll count in days or weeks, not months.

Which daily and weekly activities do you keep track of?

To keep track of shorter periods of time, we use a clock or a watch. Clocks tell us the hours and minutes of the day.

Do you use a clock to get to school on time?

If you start school at eight o'clock, the clock will look like this. The short hand points to eight. The long hand points to twelve.

Minutes and hours on a clock begin and end at the twelve.

13

A clock has a face with twelve numbers. It also has three hands. The short hand counts hours. That's why we call it the hour hand. The hour hand takes twelve hours to travel all the way around the numbers.

The minute hand is longer and counts minutes. It travels around the numbers in one hour. The second hand is fastest of all. It goes around all the numbers in only one minute.

minute hand

hour hand

face

second hand

Each time the minute hand gets to twelve, an hour has passed.

Some clocks don't use hands to show the time. They use numbers instead. The numbers to the left of the dots show the hour of the day. The numbers on the right show how many minutes have gone by in that hour.

We read this clock from left to right, the same way we read words in a book.

It's 8:15. We say, "Eight-fifteen." That means it's fifteen minutes after eight o'clock. Oops! That means we're late for school!

But what about smaller bits of time? Runners want to know how fast they can go. They use a stopwatch to find out.

A stopwatch can keep track of very small bits of time— less than one second.

You start a stopwatch when a race begins. Then you stop it when a runner crosses the finish line. The stopwatch tells you exactly how long the runner takes to finish the race.

A timer keeps track of time, too. A kitchen timer is useful when you bake cookies.

How long do you think these cookies were in the oven?

Those cookies look good! When do we eat?

People have always measured time—and in many different ways! We use time to keep track of daily activities. We use time so we won't be late.

We use time to think about the past and to plan for the future. What did you do last week? How old will you be next year? You can use time to think about these things!

How about these dinosaurs?
They are millions of years old . . .
and they're a little scary!

Key Words

calendar
clock
day
future
hour
hour hand
minute
minute hand
month
past
second
second hand
stopwatch
timer
week
year

Index

About the Author

Sara Pistoia is a retired elementary teacher living in Southern California with her husband and a variety of pets. After 40 years of teaching, she now contributes to education by supervising and training student teachers at California State University at Fullerton. In authoring this series, she draws on the experience of many years of teaching first and second graders.

24